CONNECTED PARENTING

CONNECTED PARENTING

TRISTAN EVERGREEN

CONTENTS

CHAPTER 1

Introduction to Connected Parenting

Connected parenting is a way of extracting the best from your child so that he can become his best. It involves teaching him how to become more cooperative, considerate, and helpful in ways consistent with his age or level of maturity. As a result of connected parenting, large numbers of parents have experienced significant improvements in their children's behaviour and functioning within only a few days. My main goal has been to give parents the tools, principles, and strategies that will guide them in helping their kids build self-confidence and resilience.

These concepts are built on a number of cultural traditions and various psychological theories. These traditions and theories posit that parents have an obligation to raise children to be competent and compassionate members of their respective communities. That is, the main purpose of raising children is to help them become people who are more concerned about the welfare of others than with the satisfaction of their own selfish desires. Studies have shown that people who feel connected to others survive longer, feel happier, and are healthier than those who feel isolated. So, connectedness may not only be good for other people; it is probably also good for us.

Understanding the Core Principles of Connected Parenting

Connected Parenting is based on a few basic principles. First, what we know about kids' brains tells us that they don't want to be mean and they don't want to disappoint people. This means that they aren't "out to get" us (or our children). We also know that even if they're acting badly, they're trying to get their needs met - and they want their needs to be met. They can't tell us what's bugging them very often or very well, so they act out what's happening inside. Their behavior is also the most effective tool in their arsenal. And finally, people who are treated with compassion, empathy, and respect learn sooner, work better, and behave better than those who are punished.

In practice, this means connecting first, to help kids handle feelings better by meeting their relationship needs. Then collaborate with them to meet whatever other need they have that you can. Kids who have their needs met this way behave better, do better in school, and enjoy better mental health. The approach and strategies work from toddlerhood into university.

Connected Parenting is built on a deep understanding of today's kids and teenagers. It's a comprehensive parenting philosophy that covers how to raise children and teens who are compassionate, since they're treated with compassion, who have the emotional literacy to handle their feelings better because they've been given examples of how to handle feelings, who understand that they are interconnected with the adults in their lives and can expect help from them. It translates into a parenting practice that connects first, because when kids' needs met, kids are able to give their attention to everyday tasks. Then it collaborates whenever possible. And it uses playful and creative discipline to bust power struggles and help kids (and their parents) stay connected.

Benefits of Connected Parenting for Children and Parents

Working from a connected parenting approach can have far-reaching positive effects for everyone in the family. We know that attachment relationships are the gold standard for good functioning across the lifespan. Connected parenting helps build a strong parent-child attachment, which is associated with better outcomes. Connected parenting promotes self-regulation (in children, parents, family, classrooms, and schools), keeps a threat system quiescent, allows for the child to easily access an integrative state of mind, and helps that child become all those things we all want to be: empathetic, resilient, and creative with strong problem-solving skills. Your child is happier and doesn't get discouraged as easily. In fact, teaching your children about failure and challenge makes them more optimistic and hopeful. It is amazing what connected parents can achieve through relationships. Readers are surprised when they find out that the stress at home can be transformed and the power of parenting realized.

Connected parenting isn't just for kids. Parents using the approach often find that they quickly see improvements in the way they function in all their relationships. We know that children raised by connected parents continue the parenting relationships as adults and their own children have better emotional regulation and tend not to attract stress. Helping our kids to be empathetic starts with helping them get all the empathy they need. Empathetic parents tend to have reasonable limits and rules that are flexible. When children understand limits and rules and the consequences for breaking them are applied empathetically, they tend not to bend or break the rules. When our children are empathetic, they are more likely to consider the other person as opposed to feeling entitled to get what they want with little understanding for the impact their requests may have on others.

CHAPTER 2

Building Confidence in
Your Child

The book will tackle different components related to increasing or enhancing parenting skills and providing them with essential information related to making a stable family. Parenting skills will relate to enhancing the role of confidence in their life. The purpose is to make their kids self-reliant and independent. The following discovered elements could contribute to enhancing the role of confidence in parenting skills and provide elements related to the resiliency of the children. The purpose of this document is to support parents and make them aware of the strategies for developing self-assured children. That indirectly enhances their confidence level.

The purpose of the present document is to deal with the central aspect of parenting concerning what comprises an essential part of parenting known as confidence. The goal of increasing confidence is to make the child well prepared to handle different kinds of situations, and deal with depression and anxiety. All such instances could be critical during the period of adolescence and adulthood. The level of confidence as held by parents could make their children successful and help them attain their studies according to their potential. Furthermore, has argued that parents could help build confidence in children by valuing the growth mindset and showing them that they can learn and grow. Encouraging as well as teaching the importance of effort will be an additional component to make confident children. According to , rewarding and encouraging kids' learning through positive reinforcement, making them independently solve different problems, promoting and emphasizing the growth mindset will help build confident children.

Encouraging Independence and Self-Esteem

The greatest gifts that we can offer our children are believing in them and thinking the best of them. Teenagers are often stereotypically misunderstood and are seen as lazy, uninterested, or detached from their family. Deep down, all teenagers want their parents to see them as good, strong individuals. Nurturing or parenting is a skill that we find difficult not because we are heartless, but because we are often unable to distinguish long-term needs from short-term wants. Parenting involves encouraging independence and self-esteem that work for life. We need to communicate to our children through our actions and words that they are lovable and capable human beings. We need to assure them that they are of worth because they exist. When a child's need for a sense of significance is satisfied, self-esteem comes. For every individual, it is necessary to feel good about who we are to achieve more.

We can interview the child socially to encourage independence. Social interviews with kids are a way to let children make choices of their own and thus encourage independence. The interviewer can have a list of options and explain it to the interviewee. The interviewer can explain alternatives in different ways. This conversation will help the child learn independence. Listen to their experience to encourage a young person's independence. Telling children to be independent is not as effective as teaching. To equip them adequately, we need to discuss life's practical elements. Children will also learn from their parents. Let children see the parents make choices, handle new circumstances, and adjust their plans. This will help them to learn versatility.

Effective Communication Strategies

Effective and open communication is crucial for children to develop a strong sense of competence and confidence. Books on communication often instruct the reader to develop certain skills such as assertiveness training, the correct use of "I" statements, or active listening techniques. Some of these skills might be useful in certain situations, but good communication comes from a completely different place inside. Useful communication is not something you do, as in "speaking," it is something you create, something that you are.

The following few strategies may assist parents in doing this and in using communication to build confidence.

4. Identify and represent the child's perspective to them. Listen as if you were their advocate, helping them to stand up to their own negative self-evaluations, giving them an empathic mirror to help them examine and resolve their thoughts. The more you can give attention to respect and empathy, the less time you have to worry about what to do to control them.

5. Take a position of partnership in your conversations. This is an attitude and frame of mind that is crucial to the success of every parenting approach and action. Your child is more advantageous and can think better when they understand that your limit setting, involvement, and discipline are more about helping and protecting, and when judging their conduct, simply establishing that it is dangerous or unsuitable, and explaining this clearly—rather than it is some sort of personal flaw in themselves—is the mark of a strong, effective, morally upright parent.

6. Do what it takes to make a good connection before dealing with your child's behaviour. In the same way, avoid conversation or an audience which is separated from the time that talk is needed. Avoid distractions whenever it is necessary to give 100 percent of yourself to the interaction. Taking one action in handling misbehaviour is crucial but is forecasted to rely very much on the level to which you are linked with your child and the possibility that you understand their intentions.

7. Reflect with respect. When speaking with your children, be mindful of their thoughts. Be mindful not to talk rudely to your children or to use sarcasm. Only strive to discuss with respect as you would with another grown-up family member or a friend who angers you.

Nurture Trust When an element of acceptance or "being for" your child assists him to experience a particular atmosphere of value in your family, it is trust that gives him his internal structure, strengthens his resilience, and allows our kids finally to allow themselves to confront the outside world plus life. A bond with a trustworthy human foundation allows a kid to invest his energy in exploring the world instead of concentrating on the adults they deal with, coping with possible untrustworthiness or inconsistency.

CHAPTER 3

Developing Empathy in Your Child

Developing Empathy in Your Child: Empathy is about trying to take that child's perspective, to see how they see the world and from there, having the potential to help them work through their behavior. In other words, empathy is about the one experiencing the feeling. We want to get to know them and what is going on for them in their world. Sometimes we end up talking about consequences, but only after we have a clear understanding that we have become the child in their story. This is empathy. It leads to connection that then leads to effective parenting and individual problem-solving based on what the child needs.

There is another reason which is possibly even more important: empathetic people don't want to hurt other people, and consequently are better able to live in peace. This may indeed be every parent's wish, peace in the world. And it is every child's need to be able to function in a tough world. Thus it is with peace and trauma prevention that we set out to develop empathy in our children. We are not casting our children out into the world to motherless or mother-scarred themselves or others. We are expanding their hearts to know, to feel, and yes, to cry for others. We also know the peaceful world with a more empathetic society in which we would best like to raise our children. This mindset allows for all components of a well-lived life for our children. And though it may sound a little odd to pair peace with empathy when we have been digging into the science of the brain – it is true that learning empathy creates people who are much less likely to commit acts of violence.

Teaching Empathy Through Modeling and Practice

If we are empathic adults, our children will be too. Children learn empathy by experiencing it themselves, not just by being on the receiving end of our kindnesses. Contributing to a sister or brother who's losing at a board game, helping a mother with dishes (because it's nice, not because she asks), or listening to a sad friend – all of these activities build empathy. Too often, we look for "big" opportunities to cause empathy, helping a child do a good deed or giving to charity as a family. These are also terrific learning experiences, but also remember that life provides these training activities moment by moment.

Parents who want their children to be empathic need to model empathy. The expression of our empathy will coach children how it feels to be a caring person. If these expressions come from our heart, children will understand that this is just something we do. Experiences also build empathy, so opportunities for empathy are great teachers. Too often, parents hope that spending time with seriously ill children at, say, a hospital will cause empathy. While the experience is a great learning one, let's not forget that empathy also grows from small seeds of caring and compassion. Children can volunteer only so many hours at a hospital in a week, but they can care daily for a baby brother or sister who needs help. Both opportunities, if framed correctly, are learning experiences in empathy. When empathy is being learned, it often needs to be practiced to have it become a habit of caring.

Empathy-Building Activities and Exercises

In the practical exercises in this section, parents can actively promote empathy in their children. Remember the purpose of these discussions and activities: to set up the child having an experience that nurtures empathy.

Here are some exercises you can try. In the first two, let your child set the time limit and guide when to stop.

1. Divide a piece of paper in two with a vertical line. Ask your child to list as many human rights as possible in the right-hand column. In the left-hand column, along the vertical line, ask them to write the age when they learned they were human rights. When they have finished, talk about what differences they noticed. Help them to come up with examples from their own lives if they are not sure what happened when. The important thing is the discussion that leads to empathy for those who did not enjoy those rights from birth.

2. Ask your child either orally or in writing to complete the following sentence and then discuss it with them. "You'll know when I'm happy because I'll be..." Even if your child feels unable to answer this about themselves, they might be able to predict what you'll do. If that becomes your focus instead, make a mental note to ask. You might like to fill in the gaps to let your child know when you're happy. This is a trust exercise and a way to help children get a handle on the concept of empathy.

3. If your child has no empathy for someone who has hurt them, talk about how it's important to be empathetic with someone for themselves – so that they don't hold on to hurt and anger. Write or tell a story about someone who is divorced and what they can do to

get over the hurt. Share it to provide examples of empathy to your child.

CHAPTER 4

Nurturing Resilience in Your Child

It sounds simple, but in fact, resilience encompasses a mindset, as well as strategies and ideas for overcoming challenges—both in terms of actual hardships a child may experience, and also in terms of the "failure" and disappointment that are inherent in the human condition. Developing resilience is critical, in large part because, from the moment a child first arrives, the future becomes so uncertain. Over time, nurturing resilience can be as important to the health and well-being of any child as making sure he has an adequate diet and a safe place to sleep. And the process needs to begin in early childhood or continue in some form for as long as you have responsibility for a child.

For children to have resilience in life—meaning, in good times and in bad—they must have a strong sense of themselves and where they belong. Their world may shake at times, but they need always to be sure of their place in it. In addition, they must learn reason and discipline, so that they are confident they can affect the world around them—call it working from a point of actual influence. For children to have resilience, they need to be able to express pain; to have hurt listened to and respected; and to learn how to comfort themselves. Resilience is nurtured in children when they have limits set with love—their standards for behavior are reflected in their parents' expectations and attitudes toward life generally.

Cultivating a Growth Mindset

1. There are two basic mindsets that kids can hold about themselves and their learning. We want them to have a growth mindset. What is a growth mindset? A mindset is like an attitude, a belief, and it helps shape our kids' identity. A "fixed" mindset assumes that our character, intelligence, and creative ability are static. It's telling kids they have a certain amount of intelligence and they won't change it, so there's no use in trying really hard or believing in themselves - they either are smart or they aren't. In contrast, a "growth" mindset assumes that our abilities can be developed through dedication and hard work. It says one's potential is unknown and often unknowable. It celebrates learning. It means intelligence can be very different in other people. A fixed mindset tells kids that intelligence can be judged and that you have a kind of permanent record of it. A growth mindset emphasizes whole person learning, including all learning that contributes to who you are and want to be. We are safe to try things, to make mistakes, to create, and to learn. A growth mindset also allows for acceptance of ourselves today as well as hope that we can grow and change.

2. A key piece of promoting a growth mindset is teaching our kids the importance of loving who you are today while at the same time working towards who they want to be - embracing an attitude of stewardship for themselves. Knowing that they have the power and self-efficacy to make changes, to grow, and try new things actually helps promote their self-esteem. In an educational context a growth mindset has become known as "grit." Studies show the benefits of possessing a combination of intellectual flexibility (attempting

new strategies, reinventing, and thinking outside the box), perseverance, determination, and willingness to put in effort. Research has shown that people with growth mindsets (have "grit") are also more resilient in the face of adversity. For parents, promoting and acknowledging effort becomes key in helping our kids become well-rounded, competent individuals - with good doses of humility and understanding of themselves and others.

Strategies for Overcoming Adversity

What happens when we reach the part of the book of life where adversity shows up? How can we—and all those in our family—face these adversities and survive their hits and pummeling? As Dr. Ross W. Greene, author of The Explosive Child, signals, "The challenge of parenting has been described in many ways: managing behavior, providing limits and consequences, instilling values, providing nurture, transmitting knowledge, encouraging achievement, reducing stress, and so on. The list of what we want for children also is long: competency, empathy, sense of self, cooperation, self-regulation, self-esteem, resilience, responsibility, a sense of play, desire to learn and know, and so on."

Facing adversity and reversing the downward spiral requires some specific strategies. We can look at these strategies as Survival Plans (which are also the Nine Crucial C's of Parenting with Confidence). We use the word "crucial" because these truly are the strategies, attitudes, and methods which will help us prepare our children for adversities in life! We recommend becoming proficient at these strategies that help your children to be more resilient. This, then, is the true support we can give our kids—by teaching them The Nine Crucial C's.

CHAPTER 5

Creating a Connected Parent-Child Relationship

To create a joyful, authentic life, freedom for self-expression, and the strength to withstand negative forces, the foundation of a supportive, nurturing relationship between parents and the kids is essential. The career and personal life of a developing and upraising child are cultivated by a loving, nurturing family circle. Connected parenting will only succeed if you have the right ingredients. Parents benefit from advice that begins with a thorough discussion of the need for a loving, responsible, authentically linked parent-child partnership. This kind of partnership, is nurturing and enabling. The authors' intentions, as observed in the first 2 chapters, are absolutely according to current learning theories.

If the cornerstone of the parenting model is a genuinely nurturing, linked relationship between parent and boy, its achievement will testify to the proper nature of therapies for years. The starting point of any developmental plan is the development of a strong, connected connection that nurtures optimism, empathy, and resilience. Let's look at 5 strategies: Look at your child with love, Enjoy time with your child in his or her world, Father, see your child as you may,

Communicate with your child, Creating boundaries with empathy. Creating a connected relationship with your child is crucial, as we discuss in this document. Simply to state a few of the benefits all added up, linked relationships that are healthier and happier.

Building Trust and Mutual Respect

Building empathy and strong, positive connections with your children starts with building trust and mutual respect. You need to view your children as whole people apart from you. They are not extensions of you. By this, I mean they are not here to make you look good, to be your mini-me, or to fulfill the dreams you have forgotten or neglected.

Your children are also not human garbage cans awaiting your words of wisdom and your directions. If you have raised your children to seek you as the problem-solver and adviser, and to look to you with awe, they may be co-depending with you. This is not a mutually respectful interaction. Real connected parenting will focus less on offering answers and guidance and instead focus on helping your child find their own solutions and strengths. Avoid being directive, even though it may be difficult at times. If you view your child as a whole, capable, sometimes struggling person, it won't be difficult to accept their decisions, feelings, and behavior that aim for personal growth rather than pleasing you. If your personal interest or agenda is not a major factor in your parenting or your interactions with your child, you can begin reforming your style of parenting. Concentrating on your child's personal growth will liberate you to forge a personal relationship rather than being the goon who lives in the house and tells the children what to do. You will become a comfort to your child, someone who really gets it, or at the very least is trying to.

Balancing Discipline and Emotional Support

It is essential that you get a balance between too much discipline and being overly supportive, and that you make sure your kids feel emotionally held and safe. The crucial question parents are really asking is "How can I give my child enough guidance and structure without them feeling either crushed by too many demands and negative emotional reactions, or alone and unsupported, with no one to help them get back up when they fall?" There are a few things to consider, to prevent, in the wonderful words of Harry Harlow, the last of the positive parents, "the establishment of a teaching process which depends on the use of punishment for its effectiveness."

Understanding how children feel, and the unique child they were and still are inside, helps parents to guide from a place of compassion. Teaching should be structured, but it should also be relationship-based, and the underlying message should be that the teaching itself grows from compassion - understanding the other's suffering and wanting to do something about it. When we understand the emotions beneath the behavior of the child, it is much easier to come alongside them as a guide. And when we have received our own emotional support, we are more capable of opening up and offering the same to others - including, and especially, our children. Compassionate teaching changes one's view regarding individual differences.

CHAPTER 6

Practical Tips for Implementing Connected Parentin

People who make the choice to parent differently - utilizing what we call Connected Parenting - are more likely to truly prevent a broad range of behavior, emotional, and relationship struggles before they start. Here are some of our strategies.

Teach your child to respond to the most important question they'll ever hear: Who would you like to be? Begin early. "I know you don't know yet! You'll figure it out like everybody else does." Honor and respect your child's response. Creating a nurturing family climate is the most important parenting strategy. We call it bringing up your "NQ" - if your "EQ" is high (emotional intelligence quotient), your Nurturance Quotient is high. The practice of emotion coaching is a must. Lead by example. Don't expect children to do, be, or understand what you don't. There is no judgment, only awareness, as the key to response-ability. That's why we don't use the words "good" or "bad." Bring up children as physically close and wearing as few clothes as possible. Make the focus "touch is for socializing, tickling, and nurturing" (child training) and avoid sexual feelings - they are inappropriate in parent/child behavior. Be neat

- but don't insist the kids be. Follow the rituals of connection that create depth in families. Parents confessing their inequities and forgiving and allowing, children allowed to speak out without retaliation, differences celebrated, objects and memories gathered over time used as reminders, while telling the stories, poems, songs, integrating rituals that come from your cultural heritage. As your children advance in nature and in age, the rituals will accommodate the changes. Complete and attach to your/your child's past by learning, talking about, laughing about, mourning, processing traumatic memories, etc. familiar background. Even very casual on-the-run rituals make a difference. The time between the stories, books, poems, plays, and laughter or talking times should be connected with reflection, empathy, realization, teaching, reassurance, concern, information - make the most of your little times of contact. Try to overcome the ills that have been passed down to you and passed to them. If you communicate this learning, what we call "useful language," it will increase self-worth and self-determination and solve lots of problems before the kids are hit, bitten, cut, etc. Allow internal motivation to grow in your kids so that the children are a source of energy for you rather than only the cause of stress.

Establishing Routines and Consistency

The importance of establishing routines and consistency can never be overstated. Most kids thrive in an environment that is stable and predictable. Here are a few ideas for integrating routines into your daily family life:

1. Morning routines: Establishing a good morning routine will help set the tone for the day for your child. Make sure that your child has everything they will need for school or daycare the night before. You may choose to serve the same type of breakfast each morning. Your child's responsibility might be to clear his dish after finishing.

2. After-school routines: Are there things that your child must get done right after school on a daily basis? Homework, for example? Make sure that you are consistently enforcing this schedule.

3. Weekend routines: Routine doesn't just belong on the weekdays. When your child knows that Sunday evenings are when she sets up her schedule for the week ahead, it makes the transition into Monday morning easier. If your family does laundry on Saturdays, let your kids know that everyone will be doing their part to get this task done, perhaps by having them strip their beds and bring down their sheets. Think about what you can do to make the weekend flow better.

Consistency: A tree is only as strong as its root system, and your child's ability to trust and depend on you is no different. Are there areas of your life that you can be more consistent in? If so, start in those areas. When you say you are going to do something, either positive or negative, do you follow through? Whether you have time to read four bedtime stories or only one, make sure that, whenever possible, you have a good time doing what you promised. If you have to discipline, give the minimum consequence you established.

Managing Screen Time and Technology Usage

Connected Parenting is not prescriptive about technology do's and don'ts, but it does offer suggestions for how to enhance technology usage in a way that is consistent with our approach. Even kids who are old enough to use web browsers and sites such as YouTube Kids (which allows parents to provide some supervision and add some measure of safety) can easily veer off into things they shouldn't be watching, and that is why playing near your child those first few weeks is vitally important. You're there to offer guidance and explain what they see when those images and videos easily take a wrong turn.

Our modems have a "white list" feature that does not allow access to any gaming, social media, or YouTube websites but allows pretty much everything else. We also utilize the automatic time restrictions built into our Wi-Fi. During the week our older kids have access for only one hour a day; our 8-year-old can play for 30 minutes. Weekends vary—sometimes we let them play more hours (usually between two and three), and sometimes they aren't allowed to play at all. The main goal for a connected parent should be to promote a good balance between accessing information easily and using technology while preserving strong relationships with people in the family. When family bonding falls apart because of technology or when kids do not learn to put relationships and their own social world above all the bells and whistles of their machines, then long-term developmental changes interfere and spoil the connected parent approach.

CHAPTER 7

Supporting Your Child's Social and Emotional Devel

E nsure that there is plenty of time for non-structured play. This is an opportune time for kids to role play. It is another form of social interaction that fosters the development of empathy.

Everything sends a message when you are a parent. "Do what I say, not what I do" holds no value. Encourage your children to interact with a variety of people in many situations. Volunteering with your children can teach them the importance of caring for others without looking for anything in return. Teach children to listen to others and when in doubt, think about their questions and issues before blurting out an answer. Listening is often more important than advice. Give lots of opportunities for children to make choices. At mealtime, give two vegetable options and when dressing in the morning, allow them to choose from two clothes choices. These everyday decisions are important in the development of personal responsibility. Children who are given choices are more apt to make right choices when it comes to behavior and relationships.

Learn to pick your battles. Sometimes children need to do things their way in order to learn valuable life lessons. When safety and long-term issues are a problem, hold your ground. Let children know beforehand when their behavior is unacceptable. Establish limits and let them know the consequences for not following the rules. This will help them to think before they act. The development of executive function (goal-setting, working memory, impulse control, etc.) is necessary for instilling self-control. Always set a good example. Demonstrate the importance of respecting those around you by modeling the same in your behavior. You are the first role model. It is important to foster the development of independence and leadership in children. A child's self-confidence is developed through success. The more positive feedback a child receives for accomplishments, the more likely they will seek leadership roles. Support attempts and efforts even when the final outcome is not positive. We learn through our mistakes.

Encouraging Healthy Peer Relationships

Connected kids have healthy peer relationships. According to the book, the connection with peers is just as important to a child as the relationship with their primary caregiver. How do parents help children to "stand up for themselves in resilient ways"? Here are a few recommendations: To start off, children may be a bit shy, so helping them to break the ice by coming up with conversation starters or helping them to dream up what games would be best for various people at the party might help. Parents could discuss in advance what children's options are when they don't want to join the pack. Hang around the troupe or play in a different place? How do they rejoin people after a break from the group? Parents can help children by giving the child an understanding of what other kids might feel like when they are rejected by being with a struggling play-date—such as when they feel really ashamed, helpless, and uncomfortable—and that doing something to help is a good thing.

There might be "a lot of kids running around" your home, Jacqueline told me, "but kids know where to go, kids know where they belong, sometimes they don't have a place to belong, so before I go to bed at 10:30 at night, I make sure that each of my kids are in bed, and with a kiss and a cuddle, good night, I love you, and I get out. Children shouldn't have to worry about that. Children should know that from both of their parents."

Emotional Regulation Techniques

Emotional regulation is arguably the single most important aspect of social and emotional development as well as resilience. The neurological repercussions are wide-reaching. The good news is there are a number of techniques to help children understand and manage their powerful emotions. The exercises in this chapter are small steps toward learning to understand, appreciate, and regulate our feelings and will develop over time to be significant tools in the personal progress of your child.

1. Calm jar Materials: small glass jar, glitter or confetti, clear white school (PVA) glue, red or blue food coloring. Procedure: Pour white glue to fill the jar at least two-thirds with it. Add the glitter. Next, pour water with a little food coloring over the glitter and just before reaching the top, leaving about three centimeters of space because if you top it, it won't sway. Use the stirrer to stir the glitter. Explain that the glitter is like your feelings and the water is your calm. Sometimes, when your feelings are very big, you can shake up the whole bottle and not see anything. But if you stay cool, the glitter will stop and the water will be calm again. It's like the way you inhale and exhale and stay cool.

2. Personal quiet place Teach your child to make a quiet place in his mind and heart. He could close his eyes and imagine a place. Ask him: Is it a real place? What color is it? What can you smell? What

do you hear? What do you feel? [...] This place is personal to your child. [...] Later on, when stress is building up, he can go there ... and maybe even sort out some thoughts and feelings from this place.

CHAPTER 8

Fostering a Positive Family Environment

Laying the foundation for a positive family environment involves creating a safe and loving home for your child. It also helps to have strong connections with each other. Traditions teach children where they are from and where they belong. They bring meaning and importance to different times of the year. Traditions can create opportunities for family togetherness. Not only do they present us with extra occasions to gather, visit, eat, and celebrate, but they also add predictability and stability to our lives. Traditions can be religious, cultural, familial, or of our own invention. They can be simple, like a monthly family movie night, annual Easter-egg coloring contest, or biannual visit to Great-Aunt Mildred's house. They can also be more elaborate, like an annual trip to a favorite family resort or an occasional salon visit together with a daughter. Whatever they are, traditions are a shared practice that reminds us, "We are a family."

The family that plays together, stays together. But what about the family that snuggles together? Family snuggles are about coming physically close to each other, touching or holding each other in play, and soaking up each other's warmth. Typically, one parent lies down on the floor, while another parent, a child, or many children pile on top. Think of a puppy pile, but with humans. When children are infants, parent-child snuggles might start in a big parent-child bed at times when the grown-ups are feeling especially sleep-deprived. As children grow, this parent-child closeness can evolve into a family tradition. Some families, especially those with younger children, may enjoy snuggles at the beginning of the evening. Others may opt for snuggles as a way to push the reset button in moments when things are going up the creek. No matter when family snuggles happen, for the right family, the pile-on is pure magic.

Creating Meaningful Family Traditions

Building and maintaining strong family bonds require purposeful primary relationship connections with your child. You will never regret investing time and resources in people. Cultivating deep emotional connections in our families can often be done through building relationship connections. In his book Heartfelt Discipline, Clay Clarkson suggests that we can bring about positive changes in our family by creating and moving through the difficult terrain of traditions. Clarkson writes, "Primarily, traditions give us a way to celebrate, affirm, and strengthen family relationships. This shared reverence for meaningful or beautiful experiences in family life forms a foundation of goodness, strength, and clarity of purpose that change the world."

So, how do we create these lifelong emotional inroads into the hearts of our children? Begin by creating at least one family tradition a week. Traditions need not be elaborate or expensive, but they should create a treasured sense of family connectedness. To build traditions, ask your children for their suggestions and preferences. Clearly, our rituals and routines need to shape and reflect the unique and growing aspects of our family. We begin traditions, hold traditions, and remember traditions. What does it look like to create and hold special routines and traditions that your child will share memories of with their own children? Some traditions are closely bound with holidays and are owned by a particular family. Regular routines typically happen as often as daily but can also be weekly. What makes a particular routine special is something unique to your family. For example, an ordinary bedtime routine might include a story from the book of Proverbs or a special time for each child to share something he's thankful for. Tribute weekends, such as "character" weekends, can be an example of an extraordinary routine. In the boy character weekend, you can build a clubhouse, make a kite, fix your favorite food, conduct a scavenger hunt using the book, The Adventure of Marco Polo. You can plan a seal-and-send activity collecting messages and memories to mail home later. In the girl character weekend, you could visit a tea place, host a doll tea, cook a fancy meal with a friend or sibling, give a special service, etc. Look for untapped opportunities to celebrate or affirm family life. Some celebrations that can become tradition include the following: Creating a Family Crest, Family Olympics, Family Progress Report, Family Sabbath, or Creation Celebration.

Promoting Open Communication
Connected parenting is about creating a secure parent-child attachment. It involves listening, verbalizing, and taking children's feelings into consideration. The goal is to support the child's emotional well-being and promote open communication within the family. In the field of communication research, there is ongoing study on the family communication pattern typology, which was conceptualized by Eugene D. Miller, a family communication expert. This typology highlights the importance of open maintenance and expression among family members. Families that value open

communication tend to have warm and supportive relationships. Research has shown that children in these families consistently score better on various psychosocial adjustment measures because they feel comfortable communicating openly with their parents.

By encouraging open dialogue with their children, parents create opportunities for meaningful interactions that contribute to the development of personal and inclusive family stories. These stories, with their unique meanings, form the foundation of shared family values and routine play activities. Communication is the key to all changes in the parent-child relationship, as emphasized in this book. It is an art that requires cultivation and thoughtful direction. Naturally, parents view play as a way to connect with and understand their child's world. Engaging in play with children requires inner flexibility and a willingness to adopt their perspective and participate in their activities and symbols. When engaging in verbal interactions at the symbolic level, it is best to start with material that helps children shift from a negative mindset to a positive one.

CHAPTER 9

Addressing Common Challenges in Connected Parentin

When implementing connected parenting principles in the real world, we, as parents, are met with quite a few stumbling blocks. In this section, we will address typical challenges parents come up against - problems like defiance, tantrums, power struggles, and sibling conflicts. In each case, we will give you practical suggestions based on "The 3 R's," namely, "regulate, relate, and reason."

So you've explained to your child the concept of cause and effect, shared a personal story about participating in or witnessing a similar learning curve, and now you're ready to problem-solve this. During a moment that isn't heightened, overstimulated, or stressful, invite her to have a chat with you about older sister/new kitten. Make it low key. There's no major rush on this beyond getting it accomplished before Kitten's rambunctious energy goes any further south. "Hey, kiddo, I've been tossing around some ideas about how sister and the new cat can work better for everyone. Can we talk for a minute?" Then, invite her input. Help her bat around some ideas, be willing to consider her point of view and see if you can find some common ground that has her seeing ways she can have a cat in her life without it imposing into all of her space. Also, by giving her a voice, you may uncover reasons that make no sense to you why she's wanting to keep the door open or if there's room for some discussion about consequences, coming up with a plan together might hold more value than a unilateral decision.

Dealing with Power Struggles and Defiance

Dealing with power struggles and defiance is also something a lot of parents write to us worried about. This is another one of those issues that parents often feel panicked about because they find it very hard to control. We often hear from parents who go over and over in their minds whether something their toddler or preschooler did reflected some deep-seated personality disorder or whether it was okay and meant that all kids that age sometimes get upset and that doesn't make them monsters.

Make it safe to make mistakes. In a respecting household, making mistakes isn't the disaster it can be in others. The power struggle between correction and correction aversion is tremendous. We can sidestep it by asking questions like, "Can you think of another way to go about this?" "What went wrong, do you think?" "What do you need to do differently next time to get the result you want?" It's a really small thing, a subtle shift. But it communicates the message we want communicated: "We believe you have the right answers." Resist the temptation to teach by making things seem logical. It's not a lesson in logic, it's a lesson in trust and common sense. I never get tired of it. A parent who knows when to bite his lip can find peace in weeks with a child who also knows when to bite his lip. Resistance ("I won't do it!") is sociopathic (literally, "against society"), which is to say, a symptom of another problem. "Forget it," and appropriately ignoring it until someone is ready to act sociable, actually solves the problem. Demanding an apology is just another existence proof that these people can force you to speak, and therefore means nothing once the revolution occurs and you suddenly find yourself the one begging to be spoken to.

Handling Sibling Conflicts

One of the most common concerns that parents share with me is about their kids not getting along. Learning to effectively support siblings is an even larger challenge when one child has neurological differences such as anxiety, ADHD, sensory processing issues, or developmental delays. Although you may have the tools to support your child who experiences anxiety to help him be more confident, it doesn't follow that his siblings will understand or appreciate these changes. Since siblings are clearly "affected others," I would like to share some useful strategies that I use in working with parents in a private practice. Siblings with a special needs brother or sister often have an enormous capacity to love and be accepting even in the face of some annoying behavior.

Understand the individual differences of your kids. Some kids need a lot of sleep, others do not. Some kids need to be moving all day and have a strong level of impulsivity, others don't. When you understand that as a general phenomenon not one of your kids has the same needs so that managing those needs is not a part of a larger conspiracy of bad behavior. Children love to generalize. Just because my nephew is a picky eater, doesn't mean that I have to be. It is helpful to see, what if anything your kids have in common in terms of personal strengths and struggles. What can and can't they change about the way they are wired?

CHAPTER 10

The Role of Self-Care in Connected Parenting

There can be no overstating the importance of self-care when it comes to connected parenting. Why is that the case? Even if you've never been on an airplane, you've probably heard some version of the instruction to put on your own oxygen mask before trying to help someone else with theirs. It's simply very difficult to have the energy, the patience, or the wherewithal to help someone else if you're not getting your needs met. The same principle is at work in parenting. It's simply hard to create the calm, the clarity, and the energy that connected parenting seeks unless you are taking care of yourself as well.

That doesn't mean that you need to be at your limit or taking care of yourself all of the time – that is an unrealistic ideal. It just means that you need to be able to maintain an overall sense of well-being enough of the time to infuse your family life with the kind of positive energy that helps all of the elements of connected parenting to function well. At the same time, it's important to look for ways to support a sense of well-being because parenting is just plain hard, and it can be all-consuming. You need to tend to a sense of what makes you happy, what feeds your sense of self, what reignites your enthusiasm for life and others. Self-care should be seen as intimately connected to family care.

Prioritizing Your Well-Being as a Parent

Connected parenting, in many ways, is about taking care of your children. It's about understanding your children and feeling compassion for them. It's about turning away from blame and criticism and engaging their hearts instead of their minds. It is also essential that you take care of yourselves so that you can create a nurturing environment in which they can heal and grow.

If you've been searching for new parenting strategies because what you've tried so far hasn't worked, or isn't working like you'd like it to, it's possible that stress and burnout may be two of the factors contributing to the challenges you're experiencing, personally and with your children. When my children were younger, there was a time when I found myself overwhelmed. I was overextended and I wasn't taking care of myself the way I should have been. I know through experience the value of self-care, and how stress impacts the parent-child relationship. Many people talk about self-care as being a spa day or an indulgence, and while those may be nice, I'm talking about the practical things you can do every day to stay healthy and catch yourself when you are starting to feel the symptoms of burnout.

Here are some strategies to help you prioritize taking care of yourself. The first thing we need to do before planting the seeds of connected parenting is to get soil-friendly. In other words, we have to take care of our own bodies and souls before we can be the best parent we can be. The good news is that you can. You can take a proactive approach to your well-being. You can not only minimize stress but strengthen your resilience by gifting your brain and body the care it deserves.

Practical Self-Care Strategies

Self-care is crucial for parents and has far-reaching impact on enhancing equanimity, creativity, and confidence in interactions with children. Here are certain strategies, classified into three types – Attending to: promoting optimal personal functioning; Replenishing: assisting with managing stress; and Supporting: enhancing family wellness and caring for children.

Practical Self-Care Strategies Attending to • Mindful Attention – Integrate awareness techniques such as mindful breathing, open monitoring, and body scans into your everyday routine. Keep bread crumbs as an anchor. • Learning (or Re-engaging with) Techniques for Personal Problem-Solving - Engaging in a hobby or pursuit of a talent outside one's adult identity is energizing.

Replenishing • Exercise – At least twice a week, engage in 15-45 minute cardiovascular workouts. • Tidy the Chaos - Take five minutes at critical transition points during the day when counseling children between the hours of 1:00 p.m. and 4:00 p.m. to do a quick tidy-up in order to create some psychic space for you. And keep in mind that the dust bunnies will be there in the morning for you! Also, before going to bed, planning the next day can be a clarifying and freeing process, making the "To-Do" list before nighttime to clean the mind of annoying intrusive thoughts. Many parents report that a mental shift also occurs when vague worries become specific, manageable steps.

CHAPTER 11

Conclusion and Reflections on Connected Parenting

In exploring connected parenting, we have discussed key principles such as positive parenting and the importance of attachment. Further, we have contemplated what it means to be your authentic self as a parent and to raise children who feel loved unconditionally and accepted for who they are. Lastly, we have looked at practical and concrete strategies for finding creative ways to provide choices, alternatives, and control. Time will determine if connected parenting will stand the test of time, if it is applicable in all types of families and children, or if it works for everyone. What is my sole bias? What framework have I built? At its essence, I believe that we all long for connection, that we all want to feel safe and loved. If we approach life from this stance, not only as parents, but also as human beings, we are on the path to happiness. Being a connected parent in many cases can bring both you and your children an enduring sense of happiness.

In conclusion, connected parenting is about providing comments like these. It is about raising a child who feels loved and accepted for who he is. Families that do this understand the subtleties and understand the importance of meanings and attachments. It is about growing children who have inner knowing and trust themselves, and knowing they don't have to hurry or please because their Elohim wants it and loves them. It is about raising empathic and compassionate children who have conflict resolution and problem-solving skills, and will be able to adapt to life's ups and downs with a hopefulness that 'they can handle whatever comes their way'. A child who matters and has worth will grow to have healthier relationships; both personal and professional. This is good for a child, and it is good for a community and ultimately for the world.

Milton Keynes UK
Ingram Content Group UK Ltd.
UKHW040815051024
449151UK00004B/225